I'm always imm......,.... ...... the magazines stating that they can 'get you the boy of your dreams in nine crafty steps!' It sounds excellent because as most people know, teenage romance is one of the most complicated, hurtful and involving experiences, so a fail-safe plan to happiness is like a dream come true. The articles themselves *are* helpful – if you're five foot seven inches with size five to seven feet, weigh around eight stone and the boy you're after happens to like you. What if you go up to him, start talking and he walks off laughing to tell everyone that that ugly/fat/lanky girl over their just tried to chat him up? There'll be very little chance to use the fluent body language the magazines assured you would make him fall at your feet!

Okay, so we all know the way you look *shouldn't* matter, but magazines just pretend that there aren't other pressures involved. They only use very general, misleading advice like: 'If he can't appreciate you the way you are, then leave him. There are plenty more fish in the sea.' Yeah ... and they're all in the same shoal, aren't they?

from The Women's Press

Jane Waghorn has taught English and drama at a number of London secondary schools over the last twenty years, and at the Sixth Form Centre of the Community College Hackney since 1989. She is the editor of *Through Thick and Thin: Young Women Talk Relationships* (Livewire, 1996). She lives in Stoke Newington, North London, with her husband and two daughters.

A Message for the Media

Young Women Talk

Jane Waghorn, editor

LiveWiRE

First published by Livewire Books, The Women's Press Ltd, 1999
A member of the Namara Group
34 Great Sutton Street, London EC1V 0LQ

British Library Cataloguing-in-Publication Data
A catalogue record for this book is available from the British Library.

ISBN 0 7043 4950 7

Typeset in 11/13pt Bembo by FSH Ltd, London
Printed and bound in Great Britain by Cox & Wyman Ltd, Reading, Berkshire

To Alex, Sean, Peter, Dave and Erica

Acknowledgements

I would like to warmly thank all the contributors to this book. I would also like to thank Kirsty Dunseath, from The Women's Press, for doing such an excellent job; and to say a special thank you (and farewell) to Kathy Gale, who has supported my work, and whose encouragement has been invaluable.

Contents

Introduction

TV and radio shows, music, magazines, books, and films. In one way or another we are all exposed to the mass media, and what it says to us individually and collectively has a huge impact. Young women are avid consumers of the media, and what prompted this collection of writing was my interest in finding out how they feel about the messages they are receiving today. I was a 'child of the sixties' when both the news and entertainment media were doggedly conservative and determined to keep women firmly in their domestic place. When I was in my late teens I assumed the precarious position, probably recognised by many of my contemporaries, of leading an ideological double life. On the one hand, I was desperate to emulate what the mass media was promoting as the desirable, worthwhile woman; on the other, the reality of such a shallow existence seemed deeply depressing and I strove to keep my distance at all costs. As a result, I look back on my teenage years as a series of prickly episodes of embarrassment. Developing an identity of my own as far as fashion, music and politics were concerned was seriously hindered by the suffocating stereotypes which filled the pages of women's magazines, sitcoms, the news, adverts and movies. (Emulating a gorgeous but practically mute James Bond 'girl', or a saintly but sexless Mary Poppins were impossible options for a variety of reasons!)

Fashion was a particularly tortuous area. I'll never forget the night I proudly wore my mum-made brown and cream curtain-look-a-like hot pants, with a pair of black, shiny platform shoes. I entered my local youth-club disco, only to realise that hot pants had just become yesterday's news. My 'best' friend heaved with laughter for *far* too long, and the final straw came when the platform heel of my left shoe fell off, leaving me struggling to keep my balance as I crept out the back entrance.

Another highlight was the evening of my first date, when I went to see Uriah Heep at the Rainbow in Finsbury Park. Instead of wearing something easy and comfortable, I decided to dress up for *him*, and itched unbearably all the way through the concert, as I coped with wearing nylon tan-coloured tights, in temperatures soaring into the 80s. I was utterly preoccupied with relieving the agony of the itches, trying not to get sweaty palms in case he held my hand, and (oh yes) making sure I looked really into the music because I'd said I loved the band when he asked me if I was interested in going with him!

At this point in my life the idea of confidently expressing or even knowing my own preferences for music seemed impossible. The DJs and *Top of the Pops* presenters were nearly all male, and images of Woodstock and other festivals, seemed to be all about women going topless and men ignoring them (at least while the bands played) because they were so into the sounds. Today it's a different story. Girls confidently make their own decisions, not only about music but about a host of other things. Parts of the media have responded positively, and caught up with their female audience, others lag woefully behind, as the contributors of this book make clear.

We now have a whole spate of American sitcoms which present us with images of strong, assertive young women. *Moesha, Sister Sister, Sybil, Ellen, Roseanne, Sabrina*, all portray girls and women who break the rules. It's great to see clever, bold, amusing females living life for themselves, and kicking against traditional modes of behaviour deemed as 'feminine'. I'm delighted to see females in lead roles who are strong individuals. However, these sitcoms are limited, and hardly counteract much of the more obviously reactionary elements of the media that still abound. The mass media, in essence, perhaps hasn't changed its message that much in terms of gender. What has changed is the receivers of such messages. The generation of young women today are wiser to what they get fed through the TV, on the radio, on the Net, and in films. They have strong opinions and are prepared to voice them.

This book is a celebration of how much things have moved on. As well as the representation of gender, a variety of topics are covered from how bullying is tackled on children's TV, to fantasies on the Net. The contributors writing in this collection 'read' media messages astutely, and are able to say what they think with lots of intelligence, humour and passion, without being intimidated by a world which is still remarkably fearful of the feminine voice.

Jane Waghorn

Soaps 'n' Jobs

Youth unemployment in Britain is a real problem. It signals frustration and disappointment for many, and for a few it signifies crime and intense depression. Luckily, however, the BBC offers a vision of hope to Britain's unemployed youth twice a day, five times a week with *Neighbours*, and three times a week with a double dose on Sundays of *EastEnders*. First, let's visit Australia and *Neighbours*.

This soap is living attestation, if ever there was, that the words 'youth' and 'employment' don't have to be as far apart as we pommie pessimists often like to make out. Indeed the words 'unemployment' and 'despondency' are about as alien to the youth of Ramsey Street as their opposites are to many of the teenagers who live in real Melbourne, where one person in four lives on state benefit and teenage unemployment runs at almost 40 per cent.

So kids, discard your crowbars and graffiti cans and instead exult in the knowledge that if ever you visit Ramsey Street, you will immediately become great friends with your newly acquired neighbours, find some top-rate dwelling place *and* be fixed up with a job by someone, who just happens to be looking for an extra worker! Oh, and never mind the need for boring, rigorous interviews, necessary qualifications and so on, as such mundane formalities mean nothing to the good folk of Ramsey Street when it comes to helping out their indigent youth. (Judging from the response to my request for a mop handle I once had to beg from my neighbour here in London, I shudder to think what her reaction would be if I dared ask for a job.)

Beneath its facade of good neighbourliness, however, it is apparent there are certain criteria to be met. The only way to enter the street as a youth is as a thug who squanders his talent by graffiting garages, or a thief who steals from sweet old ladies' shops. If you pass the test of suitable delinquency, then you can be processed efficiently, until you are back on the straight and narrow. All former inclinations towards crime and deviancy are lost forever in favour of obligatory shifts at the coffee shop or 'Chez, Chez', and in true *Neighbours* style it works every time. (Tut-tut, and there was I thinking that youth unemployment was rife in Australia – I ought to get my facts right.)

Yes, forget juvenile detention centres as Ramsey Street beats them, hands tied and eyes closed when it comes to reforming wayward teenagers. Indeed, all it takes is the mandatory pep talk of, 'Look, you're a good kid, I know you didn't mean to set my house on fire and you'll not have to worry as I'll not dob you into the police – instead you can stay with me until you get yourself sorted,' and a new and improved kid emerges before your very eyes.

If I was to commit any criminal act towards my neighbour; and she was so forgiving, I would expect her uncharacteristic decision to be a result of some sort of intoxicating or narcotic substance. Her judgement would have *had* to be impaired because normally the perils, agonies, and vulnerabilities of my youth would mean nothing to her. So much for love and forgiveness – the only biblical echoes I would hear would be in the severe curses thrown at me in decibels loud enough to wake the dead. As for moving into her house? Well, I probably would get new accommodation but it's more likely to be the kind that serves up sloppy porridge for breakfast.

Even though British soaps seem unable to offer the same euphoric idyll as our Australian cousins, all is not lost. True, the rain and often crime-soaked streets of Walford are not quite as pleasing to the eye, and juvenile crime features more prominently than in Ramsey Street, but strip away this exterior, and things really aren't that bad. Let's take the wonderkid Tony Hills, ex-drug pusher and now reporter for the local rag. Prior to this, his journalistic knowledge was such that he probably thought the word 'broadsheet' meant a particular sized note-pad, and his only interest in current affairs was his contribution to the Colombian economy. Yet, before anyone could say CV, he'd jacked the smack and was hobnobbing with Fleet Street wannabes and local government big wigs – all without any previous experience. See where determination can get you? I mean, and I'm not being sanctimonious here, the nearest

I've ever come to any sort of drug pushing is chucking some Panadol to a friend with a nasty headache, yet the few jobs that come my way are almost always preceded by nights of agonising over the nth version of my CV, grovelling, traipsing around London, and bouts of sobbing at my uselessness as a person. Tony Hills, you're an angel – I will tear up my CV right now – who needs one? I'll just impress employers with my youthful optimism and ambition. I mean, that must be the only thing that swung it for Tony, eh?

Ian Beale, from the same East End soap is another shining example to us all. Despite the fact that he has faced more hurdles than Colin Jackson, he is now the Richard Branson of the East End. But life wasn't always as rosy for our Ian was it? Let me take you back a few years . . . He left school after his GCSEs, his wife had an affair with his cousin, then walked out on him, taking the children with her. She came back, did more of the same, only this time kidnapped the offspring and arranged to have Ian killed. His dad died tragically and he continued to struggle with a string of dead-end, no hope businesses. In the end though, despite the fact he is as bitter as a lemon, he has muddled through and is now the proud owner of a string of fish and chip shops. Hard to swallow? Yes! How did he get the bank to lend him the money when his 'credentials' were nothing but a string of failures and liabilities? What does he know about business anyway? What does he *do* all day, sporting the suit and briefcase?

The writers of the soap seem to be saying, 'give him a career, but forget about the boring practicalities'. At least *Neighbours* doesn't pretend to be presenting anything other than a cardboard cut-out version of the world of work. The producers of *EastEnders* would like us to believe that what they're coming up with is true to life! I know that neither soaps nor anything else can ever be 'realistic' and I don't expect soaps to act as social documents, as they can never be anything more than a specific TV genre. What gets me is the sense that the producers *think* they are creating 'realistic' and 'true to life' storylines. If this were the case, a lot more of us could be jubilant in the knowledge that there's no need for a trip to the job centre, all we need to do is be a bit more innovative and employment, indeed a fulfilled life in every way, will be a lot closer at hand. Here's hoping...

Nkem Ijeh

A Message for the Media

One of the most disturbing styles in fashion is heroin-chic. Women are made up to look ill and wasted. This is supposedly glamorous. Perhaps these images may have some artistic value of their own, but when you make the connection to the fact that they are being used to advertise and sell products, the impact is shocking. If this look has the power to sell things, then the suggestion is that it must be cool, attractive and appealing to be under-weight. The world of fashion and advertising has portrayed the skinny figure as an ideal for many years, and this has become even more pronounced with the birth of 'the waif'. It seems that the innocence of a child's body with a woman's experience is considered an irresistibly sexy combination. But these images are not about, or for, *real* women since they undermine and devalue the changes that young women go through as they mature.

The message is that as soon as you start developing physically into a grown woman you are past your sell-by date. For you to continue being beautiful, your development has to reverse.

The fashion and advertising industries have come under a lot of criticism as a result of this, because so many young models have suffered serious health problems struggling to keep their weight down. My belief is that while the pressure of the job for these young models obviously makes them suppress their natural appetite, it can also trigger off something much deeper and more difficult psychologically. I am not a catwalk model, but from my own history with bulimia I know that I was not simply following public expectations. I was influenced by media images, but I know that my internal struggle was much more personal. The childlike ideal for me was connected to my awareness and uncertainty about the process of turning from a girl into a woman. Coming up against so many responsibilities and expectations made me want to slow everything down. Terrified of making visible mistakes I just wanted to be small. I also felt that I could be forgiven for mistakes if I stayed small, still a child. The odd thing was that I also knew only a self-conscious young adult could have such thoughts. Being ill and vulnerable in this way was a call for help at a time when asking directly seemed difficult and I couldn't articulate what it was I wanted. Seeing 'vulnerable' images of women in the media and knowing they were approved of and read as sexy, added to the confusion I felt. I'm unsure whether I picked up this message unconsciously but the positive feedback I got for being waif-like certainly linked in with the media's influence on most people around me. My thinness was enviable to others. With hindsight it upsets me that I contributed to the whole vicious circle in this way.

Obviously, for most young women, if being thin is seen as so desirable, the fact that their thinness can be a symptom of unresolved feelings becomes hidden. The media industries who ignore this are recklessly exploiting the models as well as perpetuating a damaging myth about female beauty being inextricably linked to vulnerability. It is rare to see waif models smiling, they look awkward and uncomfortable and do not appear to be enjoying their bodies or themselves. They look away from the viewer absently, as if uninterested in what is going on. If they do look at the camera then they feign the lost, helpless look which seems so enticing. Some images show the models looking aggressive, but they still look vulnerable because they are not physically strong and obviously do not have the power the images suggest. Whatever the pose, the effect is to play to the imagined male fantasy of being able to protect or dominate women.

It seems to me that these are narrow-minded and negative images of women which do not explore and celebrate the beauty of the female form. Women are rarely shown as being strong, confident and in control of their lives. In a recent campaign advertising a brand of watch, the billboard poster featured a model who was clearly unhealthily underweight, wearing a watch around her upper arm. The caption read 'Put Some Weight On'. I found this particularly disturbing because it was mocking the image of the skinny waif and by inference the problems faced by people suffering from anorexia and bulimia, while at the same time callously using this image to sell the product. The poster was shown around Christmas, a time when we all worry about overeating.

The media seem to be increasingly confident in their ability to define what fashion and beauty are. The most recent concept is 'edge'. People with 'edge' are people who would ordinarily be thought of as being unusual-looking or even ugly, were it not for the fact that they had been picked up by fashion agencies. The motivation behind these new images does not lie in a belief that the concept of beauty is multi-layered; it is purely about selling the latest product for maximum profit. The advertising industry seems to revel in its power to manipulate its audience. Despite variations like 'edge', there seems to be no let up in the media's relentless worship of thinness. I wish the fashion world would discover the beauty of the individual in place of the stereotype. Media fashion images don't create problems but they do influence our attitudes, and at the moment they do nothing to increase our tolerance and understanding of ourselves or others. It seems to me to be particularly tasteless (and isn't fashion supposed to be all about good taste?), at a time when eating disorders are either on the increase or more widely acknowledged than ever before, that these are the only images of young women which are deemed acceptable.

Maya Selway

It's a Garage 'Ting

At the moment I'm really into Garage music. I can't describe the feeling I get when a wicked tune comes on. I get shivers down my spine. Or, if there's a really good bassline and you can feel it all over your body, you don't need any melody, you just dance to the beat. You don't have to know who the MC is, you just need to enjoy yourself. It's jump up! You *have* to dance to it, even if your only dance floor is your bedroom. After all, what else is a girl who listens to Garage supposed to do?

Garage has taken over the London dance scene. It is characterised by rhythmic basslines, catchy melodies and soulful singing. It has actually been around for years, with its roots in an American club called 'The Garage'. Technically it is 'house with soul' and even though British clubbers were already listening to it by the early nineties, the scene did not really kick off until the rise of 'UK Garage' a few years ago.

Sadly Girl Power hasn't really hit Garage yet. This is made perfectly clear by the professionally printed flyers with half-naked women adorning them. Women – or should I say 'Laydeeez' – are still expected to dress up to the nines in high heels and short skirts, and there's no getting away from the many disgusting men who somehow think that they've actually got a chance! Women are expected to dance for men, while most of them stand around with their attitude and Moschino. It's not all bad though. You get into clubs cheaper and usually there's someone desperate to buy you a drink. We're not stupid; we just take advantage of the blatant sexism – now that's girl power for you!

British Garage has been getting better and better in recent years but it's also becoming more commercial. The media quickly pick up on what's happening underground and know exactly how to make money out of it, putting out shows like 'Club@vision', and advertising raves on teletext. Certain raves and club nights are hyped, with guest DJs and promoters using the media to advertise themselves. What a change from the time when the only way to find out which DJs would be where was by listening to pirate stations – that was a lot more exciting! Now much of the music played on stations such as Kiss FM is 'club' music and even Capital FM plays Garage. Nevertheless, it is still relatively underground. But for how long? The media knows that tapping into youth culture can make them a lot of money.

Magazines such as *Time Out* write articles about the 'underground scene', turning the underground scene into some trendy London fashion. That is what's happening with Garage at the moment. I don't want to sound like a music snob, but I can't stand the way the media manipulate music fads, and ultimately make or break an artist, band or style of music. Look at the Spice Girls. The tabloids loved them, then all of a sudden they became a laughing stock. From singing the praises of house and Garage, radio, TV and music magazines now look down on anyone who is still into it. It's as if they've decided they have the right to tell us what we should and shouldn't be listening to. I hate this desire by the media to own the music scene.

MTV is particularly dreadful. It's promoted as *the* place to find out what's really going on in the music world but it's like a drug. About 99 per cent of the time, the music is rubbish, but viewers hang on for that one song they like, or that one pop star they fancy. It's not for real music lovers, it's for people who have nothing better to do with their time.

Festivals are another weird, media-hyped phenomenon. I have only been to one, and don't feel the urge to repeat the experience. Thousands of people, dancing in rivers of mud, damp and sweaty tents, sneezing and hunger, and of course, those disgusting toilets, hold absolutely no appeal for me. Festivals are hyped as being 'spiritual' and for 'real music lovers', but that is a load of rubbish.

It is bound to happen of course, that Garage will soon be so mainstream that I'll move on to something else, just like I did with jungle. (Jungle is all over the place − it is even used to advertise cars, and to open interior design programmes.) Music is just like fashion. I get bored of songs as quickly as I get bored of my clothes − and believe me that's quick! My tastes have changed dramatically throughout the years: from MC Hammer to Blur to Ramsey and Fen. Garage is the newest thing. It followed on from jungle just as jungle followed hardcore. Something new will arrive soon, though I can't imagine what it will be like. At the moment I can't really see how any kind of music will replace the feeling that I get dancing to wicked Garage tunes in a club full of smiling happy people.

One thing I do notice now is how old I feel when I go out. The people in the clubs are getting younger, and at the age of 18, I begin to wonder whether I shouldn't already be settling down to Friday evenings in front of the television. Is this my era? Is this the time and the music that I will look back on when I'm 40-something and think, 'those were the days'? Are the nineties to me what the sixties were to my parents? And will the media decide in 20 years' time that they can make some cash out of Garage as some sort of retro-chic? Just look at what's happened to the music of the eighties! It's a scary thought, but if it's true I can't complain. I love this time and wouldn't want to change it.

Kate Lloyd

Teenagers and Journalists Don't Mix

When a crime is committed by an adult the media treats the people involved as individuals. Myra Hindley is spoken of as a singularly warped and evil woman, Fred West a brutal and sinister man. Yet when a young person commits a crime the media denounces the whole of British youth. All British teenagers smoke, take drugs, are promiscuous and have few principles or civilised values, unlike the rest of British society of course, of whom only a fraction exhibit unpleasant behaviour. All teenagers are so weak that they inevitably succumb to peer pressure, or are unpleasant enough to pressurise their own friends to act in identical ways to themselves. Teenagers have no respect for those who have their own minds, and no young person knows his or her own mind anyway, because they are all so busy being rebellious and antisocial and making their families' lives a misery. The fact that an increase in teenage crime corresponds *directly* to an increase in adult crime over the past 50 years is ignored. Tabloids love to print stories featuring teenagers robbing pensioners or assaulting tourists, which are invariably followed by mawkish opinion pieces mourning 'the loss of childhood innocence'. But they forget to mention that teenagers' behaviour is mainly dictated by the way individual characters respond to the actions of the adult world around them.

In reality, of course, the majority of teenagers are law-abiding citizens. They may rebel against their parents by following fashions which include dying their hair, body piercing and drinking alcohol, but most are reasonably responsible and increasingly career conscious, aware that qualifications are now necessary to ensure getting jobs in the future. In fact, surveys show that far from being the self-centred, indifferent people the media like to present, this generation of young people worry more than ever before about their families, health, the environment and job prospects. Fifteen per cent suffer from depression. Judging from the way that most young people I know think, a large proportion of teenagers have low self-esteem which can manifest itself in under-achievement at school, eating disorders, or the need to escape into a drug- or drink-fuelled fantasy world.

These more difficult and painful experiences are hardly addressed in the adult media at all. Other than by writing letters to newspapers there is no opportunity for young people to express their views to the adults who directly control the quality of their lives. Yet young people, by definition, are the ones most affected by long-term policies in areas such as education and employment legislation. For example, despite the fact that today's teenagers will be governing Britain when the effects of the single currency are felt, neither the government nor the media have thought to consult them. Every other section of society, whether it be ethnic minorities, rural communities or the elderly are represented by the media. But teenagers have no public voice. (It is ironic that even though 16-year-olds can join the army, they can't vote.) Yet the media still feel entitled to describe teenagers and their views without bothering to ask them first. If they described any other group as arrogant, self-centred, anti-social, foolhardy, and generally unpleasant, imagine what an outrage there would be. But, because this particular section of society is a few years younger than the rest, there are no complaints.

If more journalists talked to a wider range of teenagers, they would find every different type of adult represented in youth culture, with corresponding attitudes and character types, from the criminal to the scholar. They would realise that just as they cannot make sweeping generalisations about adults, stereotypes do not apply to teenagers either.

The media grossly exaggerates the generation divide, and makes too much of the differences between adults and teenagers. Teenagers are just developing adults not monsters, and the sooner the media realise that their coverage helps to prevent Britain benefiting from the valuable contributions which teenagers could make, the better.

Abigail Rozenberg

Loving Celebrities

When they're about 13, sometimes before and sometimes long after, wallpaper is generally abandoned by girls in favour of countless posters of famous men and boys. It seems to be entirely acceptable that hordes of young women follow male members of bands, actors, sports-men, and TV presenters wherever they go. They learn facts about them, write letters to them, join clubs dedicated to them and visit their web sites. I barely think twice about all this but, let's be honest, it *is* strange. After all, these people are strangers and are usually substantially older men. Yet it is considered entirely normal, a 'part of growing up'. Fancying the famous seems to be as much a rite of passage during the early teens as starting your period!

There is a huge media industry dedicated to the fan which attempts to make the devoted feel closer to their object of desire. This is when it starts to get really weird. For a start, thanks to the endless magazine articles, fanzines, and easy access to Internet chatlines and fan clubs, we all know who is in love with who, and who isn't, in the world of fame. Famous blokes who are openly unattached are particularly popular... I wonder why? Does it actually make them any more available? Perhaps in our minds it does, because we also know what they are looking for in a woman, what makes them laugh, why their previous relationships have failed and what chat-up lines they use. We know far more about how we could make them happy than we do about the boys in our own maths class, and we certainly care more. Pre-pubescent boys are competing with Internationally Renowned Prime Specimens of Manhood, so it's no wonder we sometimes find them a bit annoying!

In many ways girls ogling famous blokes is the same as boys ogling famous women – except that girls attach a personality to the image. We have a desire to *know*, not just to admire. We feel that by taking into consideration what he's like as a person we are demonstrating how much less shallow we are than our male counterparts, but really we're just being less realistic and less willing to accept our decidedly normal destiny. The media knows when it's on to a good thing: we are easy bait for their insidious marketing campaigns and you have to ask yourself how much the media actually helps create the following for the latest super-hunk. Blokes can bumble along with their 'crush' firmly in the realms of fantasy, fully and realistically aware of the never-going-to-happen factor, and unrestricted by the heavy hand of media pressure to understand their 'babe'. (No one has marketed Melinda

Messenger as a really lovely person. We've had her boobs thrust down our throats but strangely enough not her sparkling wit and interesting conversation.) We females are bombarded with the full works – how many times have we read about Leonardo Di Caprio's close bond with his mother (demonstrating his kind, caring, emotional side), Johnny Depp's destruction of hotel rooms after arguing with Kate (his animal passion), and so on?

Another reason we all fall for famous blokes though, is not so much to do with the fact that they are clearly about 4000 times as gorgeous and talented as anyone we've ever met, but more importantly perhaps, they are dead safe. They won't drop us in favour of our best mate, spread rumours, or even demand something we are unsure about. It is entirely on our own terms. When you are struggling through puberty, arguing with your family and friends, confused about yourself and what on earth is going on, at least you can rely on Keanu to stick with you.

However, it isn't only younger teenagers who fancy the famous. At 18, I will still go and see a film because there is a fit leading man; watch football and support the team with the best-looking players; squeal when certain music videos come on; and watch *ER* obsessively (with, might I add, my 40-something mother) just because of George Clooney. While we require the safety of the crush when we are younger, as we get older something entirely different comes into play – wicked bodies and serious sex appeal have as much pull as the fact he's good to his mother and has a nice singing voice and smile. However, that doesn't make this bloke any more accessible to us. (We do usually realise this!) Yet the media still tends to cover every aspect of the star's love life in their bid to get as much out of the female devotees as possible.

Luckily, most of the time, I consider myself to be well adjusted, able to form normal relationships and pretty much sane. I do not (at least on a rational level) compare the men in my life to those on screen. We're talking about two different species aren't we? However, while I previously considered one lot far, far superior, and thought that it was only a matter of time before I bumped into Johnny Depp and he granted me my rightful place in the world of the demigods, I'm now quite happy to settle for having a laugh in the pub with my flawed, but real, friends.

Katherine Bethell

Forced to be Vegetarian

Look at this question in a multi-choice quiz.

If you see your Aunt wearing a fur coat do you:
a) Scream 'a dead animal'!!
b) Put it in the dog basket *or*
c) Throw paint over it.

Where is the option that says, 'That coat looks great!'? I'm not saying that would be *my* response, but I strongly believe in freedom of choice and beliefs. By being so one-sided, the author hasn't allowed for differences of opinion.

I think the level of bias in the media is unacceptable, particularly in teenage media. Take the issue of animal rights, for example. If you open virtually any teenage magazine and read through it, you will invariably find something about the subject. Maybe an article, maybe a clip, because issues such as vegetarianism, use of fur and so on seem to be popular at the moment. I have read a huge number of articles on the subject and, to me, they all seem to be about why you shouldn't eat meat. I haven't seen one article *against* vegetarianism. Almost all the articles I've read tell me that vegetarianism is much more healthy than eating meat. I wonder why they don't tell me why you're strongly advised to eat meat if you are pregnant, or under or over a certain age? Why don't they give us more facts and allow us to make an informed decision? Do they think we can't make up our own minds?

Surely, before you decide to turn vegetarian there's a few things to consider? It's not that easy to stay healthy as a vegetarian or vegan. Protein, with the 20 different amino acids it is made up of, is essential. All these amino acids are found in meat, but there are far fewer in vegetables. Many vegetarians have low supplies of iron – this is particularly important for growing children as is vitamin B12 and vitamin D which are found mainly in meat products. People should have the facts and then they can choose what's right for them. Obviously no one wants to put animals through pain, which is what many vegetarians are worried about. Most people who eat meat also don't want animals to suffer. Magazines should encourage people to make sure that animals reared for meat are well treated and kept in good condition, rather than assuming there's only one side to the argument.

I feel the same way about fur. We are only given the horror stories. Teenage magazines are particularly biased, probably because the editors think we are susceptible to feeling sorry for all living creatures. Yet most of us don't think twice about wearing leather shoes!

Teenagers 'listen' to magazines, and messages are read into everything. It's easy to see what the author of the quiz I quoted wants us to think – whipping up a wave of protest, without considering that we might want to decide for ourselves, that we might perhaps think wearing fur is okay as long as the animals have been treated properly and suffered no pain. If the media gives one-sided views, everyone who reads the articles or watches the programmes won't have a chance to hear the other side of the argument. I personally have never felt an urge to wear fur, but I hate being pressured to conform with something, particularly when the press are trying to pretend they are neutral.

These are only two examples of one-sided reporting. I know that the media can't give a totally unbiased documentation of any political situation, because obviously the producers are not living in a vacuum. However, it seems to me that whenever the media looks at a debate they simplify it and take a clear 'side' instead of presenting us with all the facts and the different opinions. It just isn't the case that there's a right and wrong all the time.

The media can be totally hypocritical at times too. Take for example the way magazines encourage people not to worry about their size, saying, 'Don't say you're fat, you're "you"' and 'Big is beautiful'. All very good until you notice that every model in every magazine and newspaper is a shapely size eight (and wears the odd fur) and there's a 'new diet' splashed across the centre pages.

The media *is* our public communication network and currently, in many areas, it is hypocritical, one-sided and inaccurate. I would love to read an article or watch a TV documentary that explored fresh ideas *and* tried to get to the heart of the truth without me feeling I was having my mind made up for me!

Sonia Elks

In the Eye of the Beholder?

Living in England I feel stifled by the media; every magazine I open, every time I switch on the TV, or glance up at a billboard, I am confronted by someone else's idea of beauty. Until recently I unquestioningly accepted that these flat-stomached, smooth-skinned girls were what we were all measured against, and strove for the closest approximation possible – had my teeth put in braces, cut down on chocolate and futilely attempted to tan my Irish complexion to a golden brown. I only vaguely realised I was reacting to pressure; as far as I knew, it was natural to be unhappy with your appearance, as nearly everyone I knew was.

A month ago I returned from spending six months in India, and was amazed by how strongly I felt my self-esteem to be under attack from all sides. Surely England was the country where women were free, unrepressed by tradition or religion, able to behave and present themselves as they want? So why did I suddenly feel uneasy being me, in a way I never had in India? I had looked forward, in the months away from England, to treating myself to a shopping spree when I got back, and buying myself all the western clothes I hadn't been able to wear for so long for fear of 'provoking' Indian men unused to exposed female flesh. I was disappointed when I finally came home to find that I had gone up to a size 14, and had to search through the shops for nice clothes that actually fitted. Obviously in England it was not considered possible that someone my shape should want to appear attractive, whereas for months in India I had been trying to shake off unwanted attention. This I found strange and confusing; I had become used to being myself away from constant comparisons with the bland English stereotype of beauty. Once back in the glare it was more penetrating than ever.

The difference was partly that the media in India is far less powerful, so conceptions of beauty are more varied. Fat women let their bellies curve voluptuously out of tight-fitting sari blouses; wrinkled, toothless faces seem full of self-confidence away from any notions of orthodontics or plastic surgery. I saw so many different kinds of gorgeous women; from the vendors on the beach in Goa, with sun-creased, harsh faces and muscular arms, jewellery chinking from every available place; to rich, fleshy housewives in sumptuous saris. Women in Rajasthan wear huge white, plastic or ivory bangles on their upper arms as a sign of marriage, and this is considered beautiful. No woman is complete without her ornate nose stud and bindi (the dot between the eyebrows), even the rich and relatively westernised. However, the women's magazines, films and advertisements present the same uniformity as in England, only with a different stereotype – fair-skinned, lush-lipped and plump.

One Indian friend was the epitome of 'western' beauty – very slim, with huge dark eyes and dark shiny skin. However, she was ashamed to wear a sari as it showed her flat stomach and thin arms, and she kept out of the sun to keep a fair complexion. I winced when I saw skin-bleaching creams being sold in the chemist shops, and though I was pleased when girls envied my well-fed figure, I was struck by the insanity of the idea that beauty can be dictated to and accepted by people on such a large scale. I realised that each culture has separate codes of beauty, but they all result in the same pressure to conform. For the first time I really understood what a farce the whole thing is. I had heard the expression 'beauty is in the eye of the beholder', but never truly believed it until then. People the media label 'beautiful' could be considered ugly in a culture with different influences; likewise, I was considered beautiful in a way I never could have imagined in England.

This realisation gave me confidence but also made me sad. Like most teenage girls I have seen several friends struggle with anorexia – at my school there is at least one girl in every year that has to be hospitalised for the problem. I think of all the hours I, and every girl I know, devote to making myself more 'attractive', when we could be doing much more worthwhile things. I think about the fact that when I go for a job interview I feel I have to wear make-up and flattering clothes to create a good impression. Of course, the media is not entirely responsible for all this – I do realise that there have been ideas about what is and is not beautiful from the earliest of times. Nevertheless I am sure that at the moment there is a particularly narrow definition created by the media, and I think it is about time *real* people were celebrated.

Alice O'Keeffe

Loving and Hating the Spice Girls

The first time I saw the Spice Girls was on a television magazine programme called *Massive*. They were sitting in a theme-park car ride, chatting to presenter Denise Van Outen. I can remember that they had lots of character but I didn't really listen to what they were saying. It was only when I heard 'Wannabe' a few times that I became interested. I loved 'Wannabe'. I thought it sounded fresh and a bit different from the other songs playing at the time. I also thought *they* were different. The only other girl group then was Eternal and I hated them (I still do!). I quickly learnt the Spice Girls' nicknames, and then their real names too. I read all about their characters, how old they were, where they came from, and other things like that.

I was so excited when I got my first poster! I was eleven, and a bit embarrassed to put pictures of boys in my bedroom. It was great to be able to cover my walls with famous young females, and my bedroom soon felt naked without them. I plastered every inch of space with Spice Girls posters that I'd fiercely collected from the magazines which were busy providing the group's thousands of fans with image after image. I loved the fact that this group had so much coverage; most other groups I'd supported had had very little so I didn't have many posters of them and they usually split up or just faded out of sight pretty quickly.

By the time the Spice Girls' second single came out, there was already a wave of people who had gone off them. It was being said that 'Say you'll be there' wasn't as good as 'Wannabe' and the way the group had been put together was wrong. I stayed loyal though; I still loved their energy and thought they were great performers. Their first album came out on a Monday. Straight after school I nagged mum to take me down to town to buy it. It wasn't in the first shop we went to and I remember feeling really panicky, but luckily the next shop had it and without any hesitation I bought it and listened to it solidly for the rest of the night.

Very soon I had spent (and wasted) my money on hundreds of magazines; bought rip-off unofficial magazines with fuzzy pictures in them; and even dished out for the official Spice Girls book. With hindsight, I now think that it's really unfair that promoters press young teenage girls into spending so much money on merchandise. Families can get into some bad rows when parents think that money is being wasted like this, and it can be really damaging for everyone. Luckily, despite some serious nagging on my part, my mum resisted paying the yearly subscription to join the official magazine club, which was just as well.

In only a few months time I was completely off the Spice Girls. It happened gradually. I didn't throw a wobbly if I skipped a performance by them and I didn't feel guilty if I missed a free poster in a magazine. I still liked them, but not as much. I didn't tell myself, 'you don't like the Spice Girls' – it was too gradual for that. I was aware though, that when asked, I was beginning to conceal the fact that I liked them. The 'cool' people in my class had definitely gone off them, so it was official! The feeling that it was a bit sad to like the Spice Girls seemed to be touching fans all across the country. In the end this clinched it for me. I didn't want to be classed as sad and I'd even started to think of myself as uncool. My immediate peer group were the ones I listened to most when the decline started. They in turn were influenced by older sisters (and brothers).

The media attention had subtly changed and my negative feelings were bolstered by some of the negative press the group was getting. When I was watching the 'Say You'll Be There' video on MTV round a friend's house, I asked her why she'd gone off them. She said she didn't like the way they were put together, the way they were targeted at girls like us who needed role models to look up to. I realised I was in full agreement. It was not a coincidence (or fate as they put it) that the five of them got together. They were the brain child of two men who just wanted lots of money. They didn't really have much talent at all, and the whole reason they were so successful was because they were pretty and lively. Each one appealed to a different sort of person, but they tried too hard to live up to their nicknames – Posh was far too posh, and as for Scary... In the end I found myself positively detesting them! They really got on my nerves and I was angry with myself for having wasted so much money on them. I was pleased, though, that I'd 'come out of it'. It was great to have more money because

I didn't feel pressurised into buying any more of their videos, books, CDs or sticker albums. I believe that the media always knew the Spice Girls weren't that talented; but they also knew they could make a lot of money out of them.

I like lots of other groups now. In one way the Spice Girls experience has taught me a lesson. If I like a band now, I don't go overboard with posters and other merchandise. I have learnt that I go through phases and the Spice Girls was one of them. I still retain a bit of interest. If I'm in and they're on television I'll watch them, and I listened to their second album the other day. I still love Emma's clothes and wish I could have hair like Mel C's. In the absence of anyone else girls my age could look up to, the Spice Girls became obvious role models. Although the slogan 'Girl Power' sounds corny, it told girls that they were capable of doing what they wanted and being successful. The Girls proved this – they wanted fame and fortune and that is exactly what they got. Although I am no longer a fan, I have to admire them for this. They are strong and intelligent women, considering what they have done and what people have said about them, and even though they no longer appeal to me, I've learnt a lot about the way you can be sucked in by huge media campaigns.

Jennifer Rickard

Teen Magazines

I'm always immediately attracted to the magazines stating that they can 'get you the boy of your dreams in nine crafty steps!' It sounds excellent because as most people know, teenage romance is one of the most complicated, hurtful and involving experiences, so a fail-safe plan to happiness is like a dream come true. The articles themselves *are* helpful – if you're five foot seven inches with size five to seven feet, weigh around eight stone and the boy you're after happens to like you. What if you go up to him, start talking and he walks off laughing to tell everyone that that ugly/fat/lanky girl over there just tried to chat him up? There'll be very little chance to use the fluent body language the magazines assured you would make him fall at your feet!

Okay, so we all know the way you look *shouldn't* matter, but magazines just pretend that there aren't other pressures involved. They only use very general, misleading advice like: 'If he can't appreciate you the way you are, then leave him. There are plenty more fish in the sea.' Yeah... and they're all in the same shoal aren't they? I mean, how many teenage boys are *that* mature?

The magazines also state that if you convince yourself you are absolutely irresistible then boys will inevitably think so too, which, frankly, is the most unreliable beauty advice I've ever come across. If magazines really believe we're all okay as we are, then why do they only use skinny models and spend so much time telling us how to get the right look? And, of course, the 'right look' always involves spending more and more money on clothes that never fit anyway. If you're tall, the trousers aren't long enough; if you have big feet then high heels don't come in your size and you end up wearing trainers or, God forbid, deck shoes. The list goes on... What is genuinely helpful advice for the 2 per cent of the population who fit the necessary requirements, becomes a source of endless disappointment, depression and feelings of inadequacy for the majority of us. Why can't teenage magazines acknowledge all our differences and *talk* about them instead of just pretending they don't exist?

It could be different *so* easily. First, take the issue of how we look. Many teenagers lack the confidence to feel good about ourselves; we think we don't have enough knowledge and experience so we try to hide our insecurity by dressing up and meeting the demands of the fashion industry. But I think you feel best when you are wearing something you like, regardless of whether it's top fashion. So, magazines could put much more emphasis on dressing to please yourself and developing your own style. They could also give tips on how to do this easily and cheaply, by advertising bargain places to shop and offering us fashion short cuts.

Magazines like *19, Just Seventeen* and *Now We Are Twenty* are designed for an age-group who can work to pay for the clothes they want, but they are actually read by a much younger age-group. (Who doesn't want to be older when they're young?) So we can't even afford all these wonderful items which are our passport to popularity! Of course there are magazines aimed at the younger teenage market. But they just aren't interesting enough, and somehow a magazine that contains advice about things we can't really cope with seems much more of a challenge...

I think that there is room for magazines aimed at a younger teen culture that can really grab our attention. Instead of telling us what a good nightlife adults have in places that don't accept underage teenagers (unless they come equipped with nine-inch platforms, masses of make-up and fake ID), magazines should be telling us where to go so that we're not bored by the childish naïveté of a PG certificate Disney film. We want magazines that *know* our problems, that give inspired, realistic advice and that initiate intelligent debate about lots of different issues.

At the moment, the financial success of magazines seems to depend on them keeping the content generalised and unspecific. They continue the myth that women (younger and older) are obsessed with their looks and 'catching a man'. I hope that one day a magazine with a difference will come out to satisfy the needs of real teenagers, in all our shapes and sizes!

Georgia Black

Caught in the Net

I'm definitely NOT a computer nerd, but I've been using the Internet for about a year now. I can still remember the first time I went on it. My father logged on and we mindlessly tried to surf. What a failure! The only site we got on was Netscape home page which advertised banks and other equally boring things. But that was then. Now I can spend hours browsing through pages on just about any subject. Personally, I think the Internet is an excellent resource and it's also a lot of fun.

Chat rooms are currently my favourite thing. When you enter a chat room at least one person immediately says 'Hi Tiki/erie345/Cyberdog' or whatever your web code name is. I won't tell you what mine is! It's much more fun keeping your identity a secret when you're logged on – you can choose who to be. You also have to be a bit careful because there are people who hack into chat rooms to find out all sorts of personal details, including your real identity.

If you enter an empty chat room someone will usually come and join you within five minutes. It's very exciting because that person could be from anywhere in the world (though they're normally American). It's great the way the Internet gives you that sort of access to people you might otherwise never meet. But the weird thing is that when you're told you are talking to a six foot tall, 24-year-old gorgeous male, you could really be talking to a four foot tall, 60-year-old female. You never know – it's like acting. Looks don't matter in a chat room because you can be anything you want. Last week I was a six foot tall, blond, green-eyed 15-year-old boy who really fancied himself. Once I even pretended to be Adrian Mole!

One major problem with the Net is that you have next to no control over where you end up. My best friend Izzy was looking at a *Friends* web page. She clicked on a picture of Jennifer Aniston (aka Rachel) and found herself looking at a porn page full of naked women. The same thing happened to my friend Hannah, who, while looking at a Spice Girls site got dragged into a porn page full of naked pics of Geri. There are regulations about this sort of thing in every other area of the media, but it is very difficult to control what goes on to the Net and who sees it.

Once you're surfing, you begin to realise that the Internet is an amazing mix of everything. Today, I tested just how wide the variety is by searching for two mad things. First, I searched for train spotting (the sad hobby, not the film!) and found 36 sites and three chat rooms.

Then I searched for sea monkeys, those weird tadpole creatures that you hatch from tiny eggs, and they live in water. I got results, including a sea monkey worship page!

With my homework the Internet has been quite a good resource. When we did a project on Aboriginal art I downloaded loads of images and information. The only problem is you can get a bit distracted, so you start off doing your homework but an hour later you find yourself playing a game on some new site you've just discovered.

My favourite game on the Net has to be 'Slap a Spice Girl'. This game involves hitting some Spice Girls very hard on the head with a photo of a hand as the girls pop out of holes. Occasionally Maggie Thatcher pops up and you get extra points if you slap her! Another game that's fun is 'Belt a Bullshitter'. All the bullshitters are politicians and you slap photos of them but you lose ten points if you accidentally hit the spliffed-up eco-warrior.

Obviously the Net is going to expand more and more and become more virtual. Soon there'll be a web site for absolutely everything and everybody – even sites to live your life by. It's really freaky if you think about it. The danger of everyone being hooked up to the Net is that it will become an obsession. People will stop doing anything else and even their lives will be 'virtual'. In some ways the chat rooms are like this already. They encourage people not to be real but just to imagine themselves as virtual characters having relationships with other virtual characters. This doesn't help people form real relationships and face the problems (and highs) that go with them. It also excludes a whole lot of people who can't afford to be, are not in a position to be, or don't *want* to be 'on the Net'. Even more social divisions than we've already got might emerge as we all log on for more and more of the time.

Already there's a whole society revolving around the Net: books, magazines, even cults. Just two weeks ago in a chat room I was invited to go to a 'cult' Net meeting in an obscure chat room. I declined, though I was tempted to go along and see what all the hype was about. I suppose it's like a kind of club, an underground subversive thing and you feel you want to join in. On-line, whoever you are, 'Guru', 'newbie', or 'net nerd' there's always a place for you.

There is also a huge industry revolving around the Net and other media have tapped into this. There's no end of books published about every aspect of the Internet as well as a large number of stories such as *The Lurker Files*, a book about a weird Internet cult conspiracy (the existence of 'cults' and 'conspiracies' seems to be a big issue on the Net). The Net is absolutely crammed with advertising and you can buy virtually anything on it – last week I managed to buy a Pulp song book from America. As with other types of media, there are an increasing number of people trying to persuade you to part with your hard-earned cash!

But ultimately, I feel the Internet is a great thing to have. It provides fun, entertainment and information as well as the opportunity to meet new people from all over the world and make lots of new friends. Also, it isn't a culture based on looks, so it doesn't matter what age, sex, size, race or religion you are. The Internet is growing really quickly in terms of the number of sites and whatever the problems, the number of people using it increases every day, hour and minute. With this kind of interest I think the future is bright for the Internet/world wide web/information superhighway or whatever you want to call it!

Larne Abse Gogarty

Laddism

The media did not invent 'laddism', but it certainly constructed and nurtured the concept of it. Put bluntly, the media defines 'lads' as young men who are not afraid to admit they like porn and football. Music, television, radio, newspapers and magazines represent them as louts, yobs, usually northern and working class. They are generally viewed as 'lovable rogues'. Lads, of course, have been around for a long time, but the media tends to pick up on a distinctive shift in society and makes it fashionable by giving it a useful label. We are then made to think that this is something new. Making 'roguishness' fashionable perpetuates the behaviour and attitudes associated with it. This seems to involve heavy drinking, swearing an awful lot, enjoying fast sex, motoring and sport.

There has been a surge of magazines for men, such as *GQ*, *Loaded* and *FHM*, which distinguish themselves from porn by being less sexually explicit and offering practical advice on sex and women instead. They also cater for other 'male' interests such as football and cars, and can therefore be considered the male equivalent of women's magazines like *More*, *Minx* and *Just Seventeen*. Men's magazines claim to cater for 'real men' and 'the man who knows what he wants'. They're aimed at the type of man who wants his fun, and wants it fast.

Men and women have long been divided by society's perception of the sort of behaviour and feelings that are appropriate to each gender. The media maintains this division by promoting what is believed to be 'real masculinity'. This kind of masculinity is associated with dominance, assertiveness, aggression and athleticism. The term 'real men' implies heterosexuality, and it therefore not only distinguishes men from women, but heterosexual from homosexual men. The lad, it seems, cannot be gay. It is convenient for men to adopt laddish behaviour to enforce their heterosexuality, if only to themselves. It is, after all, always reassuring to believe that a person's sexuality can be identified by their outward behaviour!

However, despite declarations to the contrary, lads aren't always fantastic lovers. Their sex drive may be massive ('Mad for it!'), but this doesn't necessarily mean great sex, at least not in television sitcoms like *Men Behaving Badly*. Here Gary and Tony are portrayed as lazy lovers (big on sex but not so hot on foreplay), keen on 'quickies' during the 'footy' on television – at half time of course! They are slobbish, inconsiderate, minimalistic in their needs (sex, booze, football, sleep), have bad habits, and do not have opinions on current affairs – they are generally a bit primitive and ignorant. Despite all this, they possess a certain boyish charm and wit that makes them the 'lovable rogues' they have come to be known as. Their mentality is childish, helping to perpetuate the myth that men never really grow up. The programme suggests that men cannot help the way they are, and therefore women should just accept them and enjoy what they can get. Gary's girlfriend Dorothy is more of a mother figure than a lover. She nags and complains about his behaviour and idiocies, and then indulgently forgives him. What are we supposed to make of that? Gary and Tony are just overgrown boys with mansize libidos, but none of the maturity or sophistication to actually handle romantic relationships with women.

As well as television representations of laddism, the music world has contributed ideas of aggression and anger to the laddism concept, particularly in terms of the behaviour of bands. Male British bands such as Oasis, Black Grape, and to a lesser extent Blur, have brought yobbish and loutish 'in yer face' attitudes to the music scene. Such bands are known for their off-stage brawls, their drinking, and for making brash and abusive comments to television personalities, politicians and other musicians. The press seem to imply this is because they are working class or northern, or both. Some bands have even admitted to suppressing any intellectual element in their lyrics, preferring to be under-expressive, adopting or accentuating working-class accents, and using coarse language. Partly, they admit, they do this to avoid isolating their working-class audience, but it is also an ironic piss-take on the media. Whatever the bands' reasons, laddism continues to be perpetuated by music industry circles, and the rest of the media feed off it happily.

'Laddism' is certainly a very real media message, but what does it signify to us? Where does laddism leave women? Television and music have embraced the concept in such a way that it encourages women to be laddish as well. The *Girlie Show* and female bands like Sleeper are about women who are also interested in having fun, fast sex and aren't ashamed to admit it. They are keen to crush male egos and be known as laddesses (a backlash against the idea that laddish behaviour is only acceptable and natural in men, while females who get up to similar antics have been unfairly labelled 'slags' instead). On the other hand, women can also interpret laddism as a sign that men would prefer them to go back to being more traditionally 'feminine', since men feel they are being more 'masculine'. This idea is subtly acted out by male and female DJs on Radio One. The female DJS such as Lisa l'Anson and Claire Sturgess are sophisticated, have sexy voices and sound voluptuous. The male DJs like Mark Radcliffe and Marc Riley (alias Lard) boyishly make jokes about impotence and farts. The message clearly is that being sexy, flirty and a bit dirty will really turn men on.

Lads, if their portrayal in TV shows, newspapers and magazines is to be believed, assume that women dress to feed their sexual fantasies. They identify us as certain 'types'. So there is the cute schoolgirl type (hair clips, pigtails, short skirts); the tart (very scantily clad, not really wife material, but sex on legs) and the demure, sophisticated type who is impossible to get into bed! Women who are suitable wife material remain a fantasised mixture of all three. Men are supposedly promiscuous and opportunistic, with large sexual appetites. Women, in contrast, are less sexually expressive but keener to 'catch' a man for life. The media may reflect, but it also exaggerates. It suggests that these myths are the truth.

What determines whether *I* wear a short skirt is hot weather. I feel that while I'm young I can get away with it, and since I have the legs, I see no reason to cover them up. Obviously I am aware that men may see this as 'dressing for sex', but I try as far as possible not to let my gender, or men for that matter, get in the way of me doing what I want. Admittedly, the thought of mis-representing myself to men, and the laddish remarks sexy clothes attract, have made me think twice about wearing them. But I refuse to be intimidated. In western society at least, women are less of an oppressed race than they once were.

The media are helping to perpetuate the divisions between men and women. The differences between the needs, interests and feelings of the two sexes continue to be exaggerated. Ultimately, I feel men and women are more similar than they're different, and any steps towards a more balanced society would be a really exciting move forward.

Gülşen Hüseyin

Image of Death

I'm a believer in the power of television. *Sesame Street* taught me my ABC; *Rainbow* kept me out of my mum's way; the 1990 World Cup converted me into an avid football supporter, and a documentary on children's health saved my cousin's life when it described the symptoms of meningitis, and we realised my cousin was seriously ill and needed to go to hospital quickly. What I witnessed in Cyprus in the summer of 1996 changed my life for ever.

We were visiting family that summer as we do most years. Now, Cyprus is divided, with about a third of the country occupied by the Turkish. (This isn't a piece about my views on the subject because that is not the question here.) While staying in a small village called Sotera, we found out that hundreds of Greek Cypriots were to ride their motorbikes to the 'Green Line' which separates the

Greeks from the Turkish and which was only about five miles from where we were staying. This was scary, as I'd never been in a situation where there was the possibility of mass violence before. But that didn't stop me from arguing with my mum when she told me she wasn't going to let me go out later that night to a club near the spot where the 'demonstration' was due to take place. I ended up sitting grumpily with the rest of the family watching television.

It was still early in the afternoon and almost every channel was covering the proceedings at the Green Line. It was a choice between this footage, a badly dubbed German film, and a boring documentary, so we only watched the demonstration because there wasn't much else on. Then, suddenly, I saw the most distressing image I have ever seen in my life. It was an image of pure hatred.

A young Greek man was climbing up a flag pole, probably in order to bring down a Turkish flag. Halfway up (and remember, this was live), he got shot in the neck. I sat, wide-mouthed, shocked. Stunned. I just couldn't believe it. The most tragic thing was that when he fell, he was still alive for a while. What could he have been thinking? Did he realise he only had a few moments to live? How did his family react when they saw all of this happen? The look in his eyes is still engraved on my memory; they were begging for help.

The camera stayed with him as he died — unlike Britain, Cyprus does not have a law against showing a 'live' death. His strong physique seemed limp; his determined look changed into one which was confused and scared. It was horrific.

All my family, from my young cousins to my older

aunts and uncles, were deeply affected. I wanted to protect my younger relations from watching the coverage but everyone else told me to let them see it. They wanted their children to witness the pain and suffering because they loved them and didn't want them to end up like the man dying on the screen in front of us. This man, who had intended to make one kind of symbolic gesture, had ended up making a completely different one about the horror of violence and war.

Ironically, the children adapted to it all quite well. They live in a country where the possibility of war is high, where all men do two years compulsory military service when they turn 16, and where they've seen many images of war, or learnt about it through the media. I, on the other hand, suffered many sleepless nights. The shooting played continuously in my mind. When it finished, it would rewind and play again, like a horror video. I felt as if I had been there with the crowd; one of the protesters scared, screaming, running for cover...

This incident has made me think a lot about the influence of the media on how we get our news and information. To an extent, I believe the media should present upsetting images like the one I have described, because something positive may come out of people's sense of revulsion at what they see. If difficult images and subjects are portrayed in a purposeful and responsible way, like the images we saw during the Live Aid concert and the Comic Relief fundraisers, then it can educate us, making us aware of the needs of others and encouraging us to help.

However, the portrayal of upsetting images does also have a flip side. Television and films both have an incredible distancing effect – when I watched the murder on television, I was glad to be in the security and comfort of my own home, and, on one level, I could pretend it wasn't real. Seeing images which are gruesome or horrific can make people switch off as the levels of distress they experience are just too much to cope with. There is also a real danger that we could become immune to *real* distress and violence because we see them acted out so often on television or in films. The film industry puts out extraordinarily violent films (like *Pulp Fiction*) and lots of people love them. Violence seems to be a big money spinner and the industry makes a fortune.

Making sure that the media is responsible in its depiction of violent acts is extremely difficult because everyone's level of tolerance and moral position is different. However, if the media can change some people for the better by increasing the public's awareness of issues, then that's a fair reason for dealing with them. What I saw on television in Cyprus really influenced me – I've never been affected by anything so much. I hope that the coverage had the same effect on others and, somehow, stopped someone else dying in such a terrible way.

Hara Markos

Agony Aunts

I am fascinated by agony aunts! When I browse through magazines like *Bliss, Sugar* or *Just Seventeen*, the first thing I do is turn to the problem pages. I devour every bit of advice the aunts dish out in answer to the well-worn laments, 'I had sex with a stranger', 'Should I go all the way?', and 'I cheated on him three times a day'. Wow! Invariably the same advice is dished out, with the cautious rider that underage sex is illegal. I sometimes write my own answers in my head just to ring the changes. Still, however predictable the advice, it doesn't deter me from my mission of reading every single problem.

There are more serious letters, though, enquiring about things which are less well known such as certain illnesses, and real mental distress. It's strange and sad to think that some people feel the only way they can get help is through a magazine, communicating with a stranger rather than with someone who's part of their family or one of their friends. Having said that, I think it's probably true that some of the very personal problems are written by the magazine editors to encourage future contributors to 'bare all' as this makes for more lively reading. As readers we are encouraged to believe that there is someone out there who cares.

This 'invisible' person or 'aunt' is nearly always a woman and the contributors are nearly all female. The equivalent problem pages in male teenage magazines just don't exist. This whole thing about having problems and giving advice is presented as an exclusively female phenomenon. A typical agony aunt is imbued with all the traditional feminine characteristics such as being affectionate, gentle, understanding, sensitive and loyal. When you think about it, this is really a negative message for everyone. First of all, the impression that boys lead happy, unproblematic lives while girls are victims to their emotional highs and lows is simply wrong. Boys *and* girls both have problems, and some are more sensitive than others. If girls are presented as such needy and vulnerable beings then what are the girl readers meant to make of that? (Or the boy readers for that matter?) Do the girls resign themselves to the idea that they are more prone to having problems and making mistakes than boys? Do the boys have to bury their fears even further underground because they can't see themselves represented as anything other than fighting fit and horny?

Recently my passion for problem pages has turned to newspapers and adult magazines. These publications actually include 'agony uncles' as well as aunts. The uncle will usually exhibit the 'masculine' traits of being assertive, dominant, forceful, and self-reliant. This 'wise' man is somehow more worldly than his female counterpart; while she concentrates on the emotional aspect of her reader's dilemma, he regales them with positive action points which will solve the problem.

The *Sun* newspaper seems to have a continual flow of letters asking for advice about cheating partners. The advice is, without exception, tediously repetitive and predictable without much sense that real people and relationships are being discussed. I suppose it has to be like this considering the aunt or uncle has no real idea of who they are replying to. These letters become representations of a variety of people's situations which the *Sun*, and other publications like it, can then spend time commenting on, the object of the exercise being to entertain the huge captive audience of which I am a part.

However genuine the writer of the letter might be, the decision to write to an anonymous uncle/aunt in a newspaper *has* to be a mistake. It's addictive reading and sometimes a good laugh, but really it's about exploiting people with problems rather than helping them. Girls and women in particular can get conned. It perpetuates the idea that to be female is to be dependent on advice from others. I think it's true that most girls and women tend to share their problems more openly than boys and men, and they do want to know what others think. But I would like the message from the publications to be much more positive and encouraging. Girls need to be confident that they are perfectly capable of being themselves and making their own judgements. If they had this confidence, they would feel more positive about asking for help from people they know, and wouldn't need to scan the problem pages looking for comparisons and reassurances. The quality women's magazines such as *Elle* no longer bother with a problem page at all. I think this is the right step forward.

Behice Ergen

Women in the World of Films

Picture the scene: a supposedly helpless, beautiful woman has ventured foolishly into a cellar whilst investigating a strange noise. Then, from the shadows a hideously foul creature jumps out in front of her, reaching for her virgin white neck. How does she respond? Does she pathetically cry for help, flutter her eyelashes to get rid of her tears and pray to be rescued by the first available knight in shining armour? Or does she deliver the monster a powerful kick before pushing his helpless body to the ground and making her own dramatic escape? In the nineties, the answer could be either.

Heroines have undergone many changes. In earlier days it was really important for them to have a stunning figure, be glamorous and, most importantly, to be sexy and innocent at the same time; a feeble female in need of rescue by some macho hero.

Today, heroines can have a lot more fun. Women are no longer simply the 'love interest' in a film, and they are certainly far from innocent and helpless! Traditional notions of beauty are still important, but there is an emphasis on the heroine having brains too. The ideal seems to be an intelligent heroine who also looks fantastic in a mini skirt.

In many ways I don't object to this, perhaps because I am so used to it, but also because I think the unusual beauty of the actors (male and female), adds to the fantasy element of the film, and therefore to the enjoyment. Beauty is used more as bait to get people to see the film, than to add to its contents. We like to imagine ourselves in the shoes of the characters, and aspire to the perfect life which only 'beautiful people' seem to achieve.

Although the emphasis on beauty seems to be as important now as in the past, the novelty (and powerful draw) of adding brains to beauty has encouraged script-writers and producers to do away with the obvious 'bimbo', which is a good thing. The nineties woman seems able to do anything, and takes whatever comes her way in her stride. Even women's roles in predominantly male genres, such as the action movie, have developed. Stunt *women* are more and more common as female characters fling themselves from buildings, throw themselves at moving cars and into the path of various natural disasters such as volcanoes and tornadoes. Look at the new 'Bond Girl'. In the older Bond movies the women were beautiful, glamorous, and occasionally daring, but they all ended up being rescued by James in his flashy sports car. The nineties Bond girl is independent and far more intelligent. But it is still the case that, in the end, Bond takes the lead and the woman inevitably falls for his smooth charm. Some things will never change...I suppose this kind of portrayal continues because the film makers know it still holds appeal. They'll allow their modern heroine 'balls' but only as long as she doesn't get in the way of the men. It is a conservative view, and it's a shame film-makers don't take more risks because I think audiences would enjoy seeing females rescuing the good guys and chasing the baddies in flashy cars of their own. It would be original, and might even increase the ratings!

More interesting experimentation with gender roles can be seen in the changing role of women in horror films. Traditionally women were nearly always the victims, being eaten alive by terrifying swamp monsters, killed by psychopaths and axe murderers, or having their necks nibbled at by hungry vampires. The main requirement for an actress was an ability to scream loudly and look vulnerable from most camera angles. Today horror films are more intricate and sophisticated. With films like *Scream* and *Blade*, more is asked of the heroine. She still screams (and who can blame her!) but now uses her sharp mind to eliminate the 'nasties'.

Psychological thrillers such as *Silence of the Lambs* have also boosted the importance of strong female characters and, I think, offer a far more satisfactory female role for both the actress and the audience. Jodie Foster was really convincing in this film and is one of the best female actresses of the nineties. Not only is she a very popular and talented performer who has won many awards, but she has also directed several films herself. This is new ground since there are very few female directors. Even films about women, made for women – a so-called 'Chick Flick' – are mostly directed by men. This unchartered territory is perhaps where women should head next. It would inevitably lead to more choice for the viewer, and we can only gain from the increasing number of varied portrayals of women which would come with women taking leading roles within the film industry – both behind the cameras and on the screen.

Melanie Lewis

Bullying on TV

Have you ever come home after a hard day of school work, and switched on the TV, only to be bombarded with images of older teenagers threatening younger ones? Or, of a group of children ganging up on a single child? Although there has been lots of controversy recently about the amount of kissing and hugging teenagers get up to on TV, it seems that bullying is an acceptable topic to explore relentlessly. But what about the effect of all this on young viewers? The message seems to be that bullying is normal, a fact of life, and that means it's okay.

An episode of a popular series called *Byker Grove* really brought this home to me. Let me set the scene: a beautiful young girl accepts some money to become captain of a synchronised swimming group. The other teenagers who go to the same swimming group do not agree with this. Meanwhile a local youth club organises a snooker championship to raise some money. The beautiful girl chooses her best dress to attend but another girl soaks it in shampoo. The beautiful girl finds out and complains to girl B that girl A has been mean to her. Girl B offers to wash the dress. It goes on a bit like this, making it clear to the viewer that everyone hates the beautiful swimming captain. Someone puts bubble gum in her coke can, which nearly chokes her. Someone else puts a broken bottle in her bag, which cuts her hand. She gets asked to model with a billboard at the snooker championships, but, unbeknown to her, the board has 'I am a sad tart' written on it. She finds out that everyone in the club is against her. She goes to the only girl in the club she thinks she can trust, girl B. As the victim cries, her hand bleeding from the broken bottle, we see a wicked smile slowly spread across girl B's face.

In the next episode, the girl being bullied is almost drowned in the swimming pool by girl B, the bully. When the girl brings charges against the bully for doing this, it is obvious that the audience is being encouraged to support the bully, and to think that the victim is over-reacting. The rest of the characters (with one or two exceptions) sympathise with the bully and think that she is suffering and needs help. When the victim is left crying on her own in the toilets another girl notices and talks to her, but that conversation is not shared with the viewers. Later she drops the charges, and *apologises* to the bully. The audience finally discovers that the bully was jealous of the girl. Although she nearly drowned her, she 'never meant to hurt her'!

I was amazed at the level of meanness and unfairness depicted in the programme, and shocked that this kind of bullying was being treated as unexceptional. Worse still, the programme seemed to be saying that, in some way, the victim deserved to be bullied. When watching it, I momentarily blamed the victim too, as she was such a bossy character. But I quickly checked myself, and felt angry that I had been led to feel like this. The message coming across, loud and clear, was that bullying is acceptable – the bully was only getting her own back, as the victim had been nasty to her earlier. Even though the victim was nearly drowned, it was all okay. I asked other 14-year-old friends of mine what they thought, and their reaction was mixed. One or two said they thought it was violent in a psychological way; someone else thought it gave bullies ideas about how to be *even* worse. One person felt that showing bullying on TV is a good thing because it can help victims understand what they are going through and suggest ways of getting help. In the episode I watched, the victim *did* go to an adult for help, and the response was that the girl was exaggerating her situation. This surely reinforces the feeling many victims have that it's no good trying to get help or support because no one will believe them or take them seriously.

Another programme, *Grange Hill*, showed a girl being bullied by two boys. But the difference here was that the girl turned to a friend for help and this friend did support her. Also, she was able to tell an older student about what was going on through peer counselling, and this helped to sort out the problem. While both programmes focused on bullying, only one showed a clear punishment for making another person's life unbearable.

These programmes are forms of entertainment, depicting 'real life' situations, but I think the programme makers really must make sure that the consequences of hurting another person are clear and that the audience understands that any type of bullying is unacceptable. Also, I think it is important that the people who make programmes like this think about what it's like having to wait for the bullying to be found out. *Grange Hill* showed a bully getting his come-uppance but it took two episodes and was pretty distressing viewing. What we need are more shows which show alternative situations, where the bully or bullies are not allowed to get away with it, and the majority of kids are against it and will fight it together. Isn't that the message the media should be sending out?

In real life, if a young person is being bullied at school, then they're likely to be feeling pretty depressed already. If they see their problem reflected on TV and no possible solution is shown, it must have a terrible effect on them. Victims of bullying tend to keep their situation quiet, they suffer in silence, not telling anyone, and only crying when no one can see or hear them. If fictional characters on television get no response when they tell an adult, what is a person in real life going to think? It certainly isn't going to encourage them to tell anyone, yet this is the best way of getting help.

I think television companies need to treat the subject of bullying more sensitively; they shouldn't allow it to be used solely as entertainment. Perhaps it would be best if the pain of bullying were the subject of factual programmes, so that everything could be considered in more depth. The producers of children's programmes have a great responsibility, since many of their viewers are at an extremely vulnerable age, and the smallest mistake could have disastrous results. If they are genuinely trying to make their audience think about something difficult, they could do so in a way which is constructive. If caring for others was encouraged and bullying was portrayed as a very negative thing that is unpopular and pathetic, then maybe we would have fewer incidents of bullying in real life.

For those who have never been bullied, or endured the inner pain that comes from being a victim of it, this may seem slightly over the top. But I believe that TV aimed specifically at a young audience has a responsibility to the viewers because what they see has a real and lasting impact.

Zahra Attaaiee

Bach or Boyzone?
At Least Give us the Choice!

Teenage magazines for girls are informative, interesting and amusing, but only if you're into the Spice Girls or Boyzone, and you're aged between ten and fifteen. Looking through any teenage magazine you'll find loads of gossip about the latest pop acts, and pages full of endless interviews with, and exclusives about pop stars. Editors of these magazines probably argue that that's what their audience wants. But how do they know? Surely this is just about lumping us all together without recognising that we are individuals with a huge variety of interests and points of view?

I think the media has a massive part to play in the way teenage girls are seen. They create a 'typical' teenage girl who seems to be interested in very little other than whether she thinks the members of the latest boy or girl band are sexy, vain, well-dressed or whatever. Magazines like *Smash Hits* and *Big* contain information about the stars' ideal woman and so on and this sort of gossip does appeal to young girls (I know – I used to buy every single magazine that had any word of Take That in it). But there are so many other things the magazines could cover as well, such as the actual *music*.

The pop industry, however, relies on huge numbers of very young girls idolising bands without questioning their musical ability. They know that the way a band looks or acts can be used to sell records and that magazines which feature popular artists will also sell in their millions. So teenage magazines have no desire to give their readers a chance to read about something really different or exciting; they keep to a boring, rigid formula quite simply because it pays.

When I started to get more interested in music, I found that teen magazines offered me nothing. As a music 'A' level student, I have to study 30 pieces of classical music inside out and upside down, from Renaissance through to modern classical music. At the moment I am studying Bach's harmony so that I can write about his style in my exam, and perform pieces to a grade eight standard on my main instrument. So, I listen to the 30 classical pieces that I have to study, and a few other pieces that I might be playing on the flute.

When I tell people my age or younger what music I listen to, they immediately assume that I am forced to listen to it because I want to do well in my 'A' level. But that is not the main reason at all. I actually love listening to classical music and have opinions as to which composers I do and don't like, just as others have preferences about pop music. Some of my friends say that if they didn't already know me, they'd think I was stuck up or a snob. Because teenagers are so stereotyped, I find myself falling into the same trap. When

I see a teenager talking to adults about classical music even I think that they're probably a snob! There are no messages from the media which allow teenagers to feel comfortable about having a lot of knowledge about different kinds of music. There are certainly no publications which encourage teenagers to learn about the pleasure of classical music, and although most of us learn music at school, only a very few feel 'educated' about it.

I'm not saying that all teenagers should like classical music and listen to it all the time. But I think there should be much more mention of the wide variety of music, even in teeny-bopper magazines. At the moment they all seem to say the same each week and are indistinguishable from each other as publications. There should be reviews about all kinds of music – rock, classical, hip hop, soul and so on – written in a way which interests the teenage market. I think this hasn't happened yet because teenagers are stereotyped so rigidly by the media. It makes me angry that we can be so easily duped; easy fodder for the business world to make money out of. At the very least I think the music-magazine industry could make more of an effort. Since it clearly has the power to 'create' interest in certain bands and singers, why not use this to broaden readers' horizons and allow teenagers to see that it is okay to be more flexible in the way they think about music and the interest and knowledge they have in it.

Melanie Knight

The Media and Islam

In June 1995, an American government building in Oklahoma City was bombed, an atrocious act of terrorism which killed many innocent people, including children. The following day a British newspaper, *Today*, carried the headline 'In the name of Islam', accompanied by a picture of a fireman carrying the charred remains of a dead baby. It was then very quickly established that the bombing had, in fact, been carried out by Christian militants. This incident illustrates a trend which has become widespread in the media – the demonisation of Islam and Muslims. The word 'Islam' means peace, and also submission to the will of God. The Islamic religion and way of life is essentially one which aims to provide total harmony and fulfilment to its followers, yet the media chooses not to focus on this. On television, in films, books, newspapers and magazines, Islam is presented as being a backward and barbaric religion. It is seen as oppressive and unjust, and more than this, it is seen as being extremely oppressive to women. These ideas misrepresent Islam in different ways, but overall they achieve the same negative result – the creation of 'otherness', and from this a growing barrier of misunderstanding and hostility.

Television offers a source of information which viewers often accept at face value, and which they may use as the basis for their own ideas, so it has a duty to provide an accurate picture of what it seeks to portray. With regard to Islam this is rarely the case. Instead, only two stereotypical images of Muslims are offered. On the one hand, we have characters from films and dramas such as BBC 1's *EastEnders* and BBC 2's *This Life*, who are Muslim in name only. These characters totally adopt western values and culture and should their religion or cultural background be mentioned, it is treated as cause for acute embarrassment. The other, and more common stereotype, is that of the violent religious fanatic. In current affairs programmes we are constantly offered the image of Muslims as savage terrorists, killing innocent people and showing no remorse. What they don't remind us is that these people are a small minority who have nothing whatsoever to do with the vast majority of Muslims who want to live in peace. The danger is that viewers will automatically associate Islam with nothing but negative images. In reality, it is rare to find people who conform completely to either stereotype.

I am a practising Muslim woman with all my values stemming from Islam, yet I have also adopted some western ideas and institutions, having been born and brought up in the west. Directly related to this is how the media chooses to depict Muslim women, an issue close to my heart. In newspapers and magazine articles and on television in general, we are portrayed as being weak and submissive to a religion which seeks to oppress and dominate. Yet within Islam we have a place of respect and equality. Despite the beliefs put forward by the media, our religion does not offer us a lower status than men, as the Qur'an illustrates:

And for women are rights over men
similar to those of men over women (2:226)

Over 1400 years ago Islam gave women rights which women in the west have only been given during this century, such as the right to own property, the right to inherit and the right to make a contract in one's own name. Annie Besant, writing in the 1930s, observed that, 'It is only in the last twenty years that Christian England has recognised the right of women to property, while Islam has allowed this right from all times. It is a slander to say that Islam preaches that women have no souls.' Women are seen as the spiritual and intellectual equals of men, though again this is not the image presented by the media.

Islam is the fastest growing religion in the world. The media has again managed to attach a negative stigma to this fact, claiming that this spread has only taken place in deprived communities which, according to them, means it is an isolated phenomenon among people they consider to be of low social standing.

The term 'Islamophobia' has emerged within many

circles and this is a reflection of the collective feelings of rejection and alienation that are being experienced by young Muslims living in Britain in the late 1990s. Why does the media choose to misrepresent a whole section of society in this way? Surely there can't be many Muslims working in the media if such stereotyped ideas keep invading our screens, our newspapers and magazines? It is clear that a lot of people working within the media don't understand Islam but there are many sources through which it can be researched, and it is a shame that those responsible don't seem to try to find out more. I think we would all gain if those working in the media made a concerted effort to present us with the full picture.

Sairra Patel

Girls Get Stronger

I love reading and at any given opportunity I'll go into a bookshop and head for the shelves labelled 'Teenage Fiction'. (These are usually located in really awkward places – I think bookshops are afraid of teenagers and think we're all shoplifters!) During the course of my browsing it has struck me that the books aimed at teenage girls are presented to us in a very particular way. The covers of these books are really similar, lots of colour with a strong image of the main character on the front and a title that reads like a headline from a girls' magazine. (I often get sold on a book just because the title tells a good story. 'How could you do this to me mum?' would make me pick up the book immediately.) The vast majority of these books are about girls who go through a variety of life experiences and emerge stronger at the end. Even the older classics are marketed in this way – Anne Frank's *Diary* has a fly cover which entices us to read it as an example of how a young girl grows stronger and more in touch with her feelings because of the horrendous circumstances in which she finds herself. The strength of the books is in the personal insight given and in the internal world of the characters – in a way they are all about our own private dilemmas.

The boys' books on the shelves look entirely different. The loud covers depict serious action and adventure stories. There are no books that look like they deal with emotional or domestic themes. The message is that boys prefer light-hearted, action-packed, unrealistic stories to 'escape' the real world. They want macho science-fiction, shoot 'em dead books, while it is assumed that girls prefer reading about other people's personal situations, figuring out the emotions the characters are going through, and imagining themselves coping with the same drama.

It makes me wonder how much we have all been manipulated towards enjoying one kind of fiction over another. I do think it's true that many girls and women like stories that are about relationships and personal struggles. For whatever reason I would much rather choose a book that explore these themes, than a science-fiction adventure story. But that is my personal preference and I'm sure that there are plenty of girls who think differently. It's the assumption that we *all* want the same thing that annoys me.

Recently I have read three books which I think highlight what I really like about my kind of fiction and what makes it suitable for everyone – not just girls. The first one is called *The Best Little Girl in The World* by

Steven Levenkron. The story is about a girl's struggle with anorexia nervosa, and the efforts of her family and doctor to bring her back to health. While I was reading it, I felt many different emotions, and that is something I really enjoy when I'm reading. In the beginning I thought the girl was just over-acting and I became a bit irritated by her. As the story progressed I felt much more sympathetic – she was responding to her difficulties by becoming stronger and more independent in her mind, even if her body was still out of her control. There is a lot of pressure on girls to be thin, so it made sense to me that when this girl was desperate for some attention, she tried to make herself 'better' by getting thin. What was good about the story was that it made me think about how I deal with things in my own life, and it taught me a lot about anorexia, and how dangerous it can be.

The second book I read was called *Walk Two Moons* by Sharon Creech. The story is about the journey Salamanca Hiddle takes with her grandparents right across America to meet up with her mum. Salamanca finds part of the trip tedious, and becomes more and more anxious about the need to get to her mum in time for her mum's birthday. At the very end of the book you learn that Salamanca's mum was killed in a road accident some time before. The book demands a lot of emotional energy. As the story unfolded I got more and more involved in thinking about Salamanca's responses to things. Some of her behaviour seemed to be very unreasonable, but in the end, the story really moved me and I felt it had also helped me learn more about myself.

The third book *A Different Life* by Lois Keith also depicts a girl who becomes tougher and more self-aware as a result of her experience. After a swim in the sea, Libby is struck down with a mysterious illness which means she can't walk. When I was reading her story I was constantly surprised by the turn of events which meant that, by the end of the book, she was able to be really strong and even helped her parents come to terms with reality rather than always hoping for a 'cure' that would make her walk again.

I liked all these books because the characters in them were real to me. The unpredictability of stories about personal struggles keeps me interested, and because I feel as if I'm going through the characters' problems myself as I read, I always learn something from them.

I think it's a pity that boys my age are not encouraged to read these books simply because the books are marketed in such a way that most boys would rather be seen dead than buying a copy! I do think that some stories appeal more to one gender than the other to a certain extent, but the way books are marketed distorts this divide and blows it out of all proportion. The thing is that if a story is good, then it's interesting for everyone, both girls and boys. After all, girls enjoy action and adventure plots, and boys do enjoy a story with a personal struggle woven into the plot – they have an emotional life too! The themes of heroism, bravery and courage are appealing for both sexes. Perhaps the differences between us wouldn't seem so big if the media didn't magnify them all the time just to sell us their products.

Ella Ward

Boys Behaving Badly?

The other day I saw the semi-finals of *Countdown*, Channel 4's word and number quiz for adults. I was amazed to see that one of the contestants was a 16-year-old boy, who had been on the programme for a number of days, winning, with really high scores. He was very bright, intelligent and was competing as an adult amongst adults. This seemed odd, and thinking about my reaction I realised it was because teenage boys are hardly ever represented like this on television. As a teenage girl I have got used to how the media represents us, but until then I hadn't given much thought to the way boys are portrayed.

On the news we always seem to be hearing about teenage boys committing crimes. Their identity is protected which has the effect of making the general public think 'all boys are like this'. Because the offender is not perceived as an individual, the bald reporting about 'youth crime' gives the impression that there are gangs of rampaging adolescent boys out there, all committing increasingly dangerous offences. The news reports the crimes of the very young with even more attention to detail because of the shock value, and the added 'juiciness' of a good story. The message seems to be that teenage boys are to be feared. This is nothing new. There's a long tradition of representing boys as badly behaved, from the *Just William* stories to *Peter Pan*.

In soaps the story is the same. For example, in *Neighbours* and *EastEnders*, teenage boys seem to be forever getting into trouble and having to apologise to adults. Their behaviour, and the consequences of what they do, seem to be considered normal and, therefore, acceptable. It is taken for granted that boys are badly behaved, get into trouble with both the local community and the law, and are less reliable and responsible than girls. In dramas aimed at young viewers (12 and under) we get the occasional friendly, wise, sensible boy who helps out his friends, but in adult dramas and soaps the teenage boy is a pretty hopeless case.

On children's television the message is different but it still follows a stereotype. For quite a while there has been a fashion for using presenters in their mid–teens on many of the shows. The boys come across as being rather tough, streetwise and cocky, with a strong dialect of some kind. The TV seems to be promoting a 'loutish' image which perpetuates all the old–fashioned ideas that boys have to be loud and 'laddish' to be popular and successful.

You might be wondering why I'm bothered by all of this? Well, it has a direct effect on me. It makes me mad to think that by defining boys in this way, television is making girls out to be very insipid alternatives! They daren't show girls being positive, forceful and assertive, or bullying, stealing and fighting, without there being a huge significance attached to what this means. All too easily girls are labelled; they are either mad, bad or sad if they are anything other than passive, sweet and compliant. The usual representation of girls on television is one that prioritises looks and popularity, and we only hear of teenage girls on the news in stories of rape, and pregnancy.

In soaps some of the girls can be quite outrageous and zany for a while (and they are all, of course, extremely pretty), but they all toe the line in the end, or get their come-uppance. Either way, boyfriends, or the lack of them, are the focus of their attentions and motivate their actions. Girl presenters are young, girly, highly attractive model-types who are used in a very particular way to sell the programme as something sexy to watch.

On television, girls and boys are defined in a limited, boring way a lot of the time. However, I think girls are more aware of what's going on. In my girls' school we are encouraged to be strong, independent and proud of our gender and sexuality, and we understand that the media has a very one dimensional view of young women. But the boys I know, who go to boys' schools, all say that they have never been told to be proud of being a boy. In one way maybe they don't need to be told, but I do believe that boys are vulnerable too, and when all they see are negative images of themselves or stereotypical macho types, then there is little opportunity for them to accept themselves as sensitive, caring and kind. They want to live up to what they see on the screen. These negative stereotypes polarise the differences between girls and boys and can cause difficulties in boy/girl friendships and relationships. Boys need to be given more positive images which encourage them to recognise all the sides of their character. Stereotyping teenagers in any way can be hard to cope with as we are at a particularly vulnerable time in our lives. That's why it was great to see an ordinary teenage boy on *Countdown* and it would be good to see many more real teenagers on television.

Louise Gordon

What's in a Soap?

The Fowlers, Mitchells, Battersbys and Duckworths – stock characters in the two leading soap operas in this country, *EastEnders* and *Coronation Street* – are just a few of the families we invite into our homes every week.

The viewing figures show the popularity of soap operas, but why are they *so* popular? Is it purely their entertainment value, or do they operate on a different level, helping us deal with many of the problems we face in real life? Does *EastEnders* offer a true reflection of life in London's East End, and does the Manchester of The Street exist outside the TV studio? If so, you would have to question the sanity of the poor residents of these cities. How can they live in a place where adultery appears to be compulsory, backstabbing a way of life, and bitterness and anger the essential weapons for survival? Maybe we are a nation that thrives on negativity, or maybe it's just soothing to see other people going through the problems we do, albeit in a highly dramatised way. Soaps are marketed as 'slice of life' dramas, and in many ways they are. However, when you think about the storylines and characters, there are so many things that are overlooked or presented in a completely unrealistic way.

My experience of life in the East End of London has been very different to the one portrayed in *EastEnders*. I find it mildly amusing that everyone is meant to know each other and that almost everyone is related. *EastEnders* has the most complex web of relationships: Phil Mitchell is the stepfather of Ian Beale, and Ian has a brother the same age as his own twins. Pat Evans is the grandmother of one of Ian's children, and is also the stepmother of Ricky Butcher, whose father Frank is (at the time of writing), on the verge of beginning a relationship with Peggy Mitchell, the mother of Phil. Have any of them ever considered travelling outside of Albert Square to find a partner?

Newcomers in soaps always seem to be immediately accepted and instantly known by everyone. The Battersbys made a grand entrance in The Street as the 'neighbours from hell'. And yet, despite their obvious lack of social graces, in the space of a few weeks they were totally integrated into the tightly woven community that, sadly, only appears to exist in fiction.

Many of us would like to be able to deal with our problems as easily as Pauline Fowler, whose solution to everything is to, 'have a cuppa tea', and to find easy solace in her continual remembrance of the deceased, Arthur Fowler and Lou Beale. It would also be nice to live in a world where there were so many characters just put there for our amusement. Liz MacDonald, the over-the-hill Barbie doll of The Street struts her stuff in a mini skirt that looks more like a belt; then there is Fred Elliot who bears a close resemblance to the cartoon character 'Foghorn Leghorn'. In reality, people like this would drive us all to distraction, but in the comforting world of the soaps we can laugh at their eccentricities, and be consoled by the knowledge that however odd we may be, in the soap writers' imagination there are always people more laughable than ourselves.

There's more to soaps than just giving us a laugh though. A lot of us feel reassured by the storylines in soaps. At least one of the problems they raise is likely to capture the emotions and turmoil that a particular individual is facing at that time. Many people suffer in silence and it is always helpful to know that the issue is recognised as a real problem. Many women have identified with Tiffany, and many men probably see a part of themselves in Grant. Walking time-bombs like Grant do exist. Tiffany's decision to leave Grant because of the emotional and physical abuse she was suffering, may not have given women in abusive relationships the courage to leave their partners, but who's to say that it didn't give them hope? It is to their credit that soaps, in their desire to appear balanced, attempt to explore issues such as abuse in relationships from all sides. Many men are abusive because of pent-up anger over a past traumatic event. In Grant's case, his participation in the Falklands' War has left him mentally scarred.

Soap operas often attempt to tackle controversial issues, and these issues tend to reflect contemporary concerns. As a teenager I am aware of sexually transmitted diseases. Lenny's hepatitis scare which, if he'd had it, could have infected Bianca and then, in turn, Ricky, was a brilliant example of how soaps can touch on ordinary lives, reminding people (particularly in my generation) that it is essential to use protection. The need for protection is highlighted, perhaps comically, by the aforementioned incestuous nature of relationships in soaps. Sharon was married to Grant, who is married to Tiffany, who was with Tony, who slept with Simon, who is now with Chris. Sharon had an affair with Phil who was married to Kathy, who had an affair with the vicar. The way the residents of Albert Square arrange their sex lives, it won't be long before the whole of Walford is queuing up outside the nearest STD clinic – now that's an episode I'd pay to see!

One of the main problems with soaps is when the line between fantasy and reality becomes blurred. Remember Deirdre from *Coronation Street*, who became 'blinded by love' and in a complex, and largely unbelievable storyline, ended up in prison for fraud? This had the nation in uproar. The real events that followed would not have been out of place in a soap. 'Free Deirdre!' posters appeared around the country and even the prime minister made a 'Free Deirdre' statement. Allegedly, opportunist criminals were jumping on the bandwagon, proclaiming their innocence and stating, 'She probably had the same judge we did . . .'

What is clear is that the support Deirdre received was overwhelming. Maybe much of it was cooked up by a frenzied tabloid press desperate to sell papers, but I was left to reflect, with a certain sadness, that in a world where serious injustices continue to happen, it takes a character from a soap opera to stir people into action.

If the episode above helps us recognise the power of soaps, then it becomes clear that they have a responsibility to us, the viewers. It is because of this that I'm angry that there are so few positive role models for young women. Although the young women in *EastEnders* are not marginalised, and many of them are strong characters who don't mince their words, main characters such as Tiffany and Bianca have very little real ambition. Bianca's biggest triumph appears to be owning her own market stall – great! This is, I'm sure, an ambition that most of us East End girls have. It is left to men like Roy, Frank and George to make all the business deals. The large majority of women in soaps are more concerned with getting married, sustaining a marriage, or recovering from one. What kind of signals does this give to young women? Should we all leave the serious business to men and settle for menial jobs such as running the launderette, or the café? Perhaps we should just stay at home and take care of the beloved men in our lives. It seems as though soap operas can move with the times on certain issues, but appear to be stuck in the dark ages when it comes to others.

The models of men in soaps are not particularly enlightened either. There is the Grant Mitchell model – arrogant, selfish and moody. Then, at the other end of the scale there is the Roy Evans fatherly type – sickeningly kind, generous and without a bad bone in his body. Although these attributes are pleasing, he is also extremely boring; more effective than a sleeping pill. Younger men such as Huw and Lenny are simply a mass of sexual hormones disguised as people. There is perhaps one exception and that is Robbie Jackson who is in a league of his own. Nothing appears to go right for him and although I sympathise, I can't help thinking that if he grasped the concept of shampoo, things might look slightly brighter. Soaps tend to categorise people too easily. As far as men are concerned, it would be refreshing for a soap to come up with a fully 'rounded' character.

Another glaring gap in most soaps concerns the value of education. With a few notable exceptions, such as Michelle Fowler getting an Open University degree, the idea of getting a good education to help you build a better life is overlooked. Many of my friends, all from working–class backgrounds, have had it drummed into them by their parents that a good education is important. School appears to be something that is endured by the young characters in our soaps. The message appears to be that the sooner you leave school, the sooner you can start wheeling and dealing, having relationships and, if you're lucky, run your own market stall.

The most glaring omission though, has to be soaps' failure to show that we are living in a multicultural society. Fiona is the only black person in *Coronation Street*, and *Emmerdale* rarely portrays any ethnic minorities. *EastEnders* makes more effort than most, but there is a glaring lack in the representations of ethnic culture. Sanjay, the Asian market stall owner, for example, is as 'East End' as the other residents (I am just waiting for him to start using cockney rhyming slang!) and Beppe and Gianni, the Italian restaurant owners, are stereotypical Italian casanovas, which is such a dated and insulting representation.

If we accept that soaps have a role to play in our lives, and a quick look at the viewing figures suggests that they *are* important, then it is clear they have a duty to act responsibly when confronting serious issues and contemporary concerns. However, in the end it's down to us, the viewers, to put things into perspective and see the limitations. First and foremost, soap operas are there to entertain us and they don't claim to be documentaries or educational. They do take it upon themselves to explore social issues in an attempt to identify with their audience. When looking at it in these terms, many soap operas have struck a good balance between fun and serious issues, and so long as we remember this, and don't let our judgement become clouded, we can use their portrayal of social situations to help us tackle and understand things that are happening in our own lives.

Sandra Coate

Tell You What I Want!

Whether you live in the Amazon, South Pole or Outer Mongolia, everyone, in some way, has been affected by the phenomenon that has spread across the world in the late 1990s: Girl Power! Did men come up with the idea as an excuse to see lots of girls in short skirts looking sexy, or is it just revamped feminism with a cause? The answer is neither. To have Girl Power means to be loud and proud; it's about status, opinions and a lot of 'attitude'. It's not related to feminism because it's not really about serious issues like equal opportunities and pay and it doesn't target one particular cause, it's much more about image. Girl Power is a way of thinking, a style and attitude which more and more girls and women are using to their advantage.

But who do we have to thank for this new lease of life? Most would answer 'The Spice Girls', but they have merely publicised it. Girl Power has been lurking in the undergrowth for years waiting for the right time to make itself known. One of the first people to proclaim its message was Madonna. Let's face it, to wear 'that bra' took more Girl Power than most ordinary mortals can muster in a whole lifetime. Alanis Morisette followed. Oozing youth and talent, she seemed ready to chop off the vital organ of any man who dared to dump on her. She was someone to be reckoned with. Meredith Brookes, another singer from a similar mould, pronounced herself a 'bitch', turning the insult into the biggest compliment a girl could have!

These outbursts of Girl Power are not only heard in music, but are echoed on the small and big screen. Movies about female action heroes are the latest craze, producing *Tank Girl* and *GI Jane*. Meanwhile on TV we can see the likes of Bianca (*EastEnders*) and Jackie Dixon (*Brookside*) taking control in the soaps, while the *Girlie Show* scares half of the males in Britain to death!

Some people say Girl Power presents women in a bad light; a load of trouble-makers who should be behaving in a more 'feminine' fashion. Well I don't think that's right. Would women have got the vote if they'd stayed at home ironing the doilies instead of handcuffing themselves to the railings? Will we achieve equal pay by sending our bosses nice sponge cakes? I think not! We're told to fight for our beliefs, but then we're ridiculed when we do so.

Others criticise the Girl Power look because it's sexy and striking. I believe every woman should be able to wear what she wants, long or short, high or low. If we want to dress in a certain way does it automatically mean we're doing it to please men? Why does it never occur to anyone that we are individuals who dress in a way we are happy with in order to give ourselves confidence?

This is all a symptom of a deep inequality that has somehow survived the fifties. If a girl goes out with loads of boys she is branded a slut/slapper/tart. If a boy goes out with loads of girls, on the other hand, he is a hero, a stud; someone other boys want to be like. I think this is what Girl Power is trying to overcome. It is trying to show that girls can do what they want, how they want and be proud of it. They can tell boys the score and if boys don't like it, tough. Girls can make the first move, they can make the last. They don't get sad, they get mad, and they do it all with style.

Of course, this is all very well in theory but in the real world there are a few problems that come with Girl Power. For teenage girls it's essential to strike a balance between being a strong, assertive character and a power freak, who never knows when to let up. Successful Girl Power means being able to bat your eyelashes one minute and put your foot down the next, but this isn't easy for everyone to achieve. Not all girls are strong and full of self-confidence and getting the bottle to go with Girl Power can be difficult. The girls that really let the side down are the ones who go on about being strong, but when the first boyfriend comes along, their friends are immediately dropped and what 'he' says goes. These girls suffer from serious Girl Power deficiency and are ultimately dumped by both their boyfriends and girlfriends.

So next time you hear about Girl Power, remember there's more to it than one pop group telling you what they 'really, really want'. It's about what *you* want. It's time to give men a wake-up call; we aren't going to sit back and let them have it all their own way any more. We want a piece of the action, and we've only just begun the task of getting it!

Joanna Burgin

Contributors' Notes

Larne Abse Gogarty lives in North London. She is in Year Eight at Fortismere School. She enjoys Art and History, but hates PE! In her spare time, she likes going into town with her friends, playing her electric guitar, horseriding and listening to music.

Zahra Attaaiee is 15 and lives in London with her mum, dad, and two younger sisters, Safiya and Salma. She is currently studying for her GCSEs at Parliament Hill School. She spends her free time reading, playing basketball, watching TV and writing.

Katherine Bethell is 18 years old. Having completed her 'A' levels, she is spending a year in the Dominican Republic teaching English as a second language, literacy, numeracy, art and craft. When she returns, she will go to Oxford University to study Human Sciences. She still has her walls plastered with pics of gorgeous men!

Georgia Black is 15 and is studying for her GCSEs at Cherwell School, Oxford. She hopes to do German, French, Maths and Art at 'A' level. She is an only child; sings constantly and obsessively, with a short break for food; then switches to piano playing, listening to music, or watching *The Simpsons*!

Joanna Burgin is 15. She enjoys studying English Literature and Spanish. In her spare time, Joanna likes going out and listening to retro music. She has a passion for football and is a dedicated Arsenal supporter.

Sandra Coate was born in Kent and moved to London when she was three. She is now 18 and is studying for 'A' levels. Sandra hopes to go on to university to do a Media degree, and then pursue a career in writing. She loves going out with her friends and is a voracious reader.

Sonia Elks is 15, lives with her parents in East London, and is studying for her GCSEs. She plays the cello and the piano, and loves listening to all sorts of music. Sonia is a committed meat-eater and hates green vegetables.

Behice Ergen is 17. She is presently studying English Literature, French, Sociology and Turkish at 'A' level. She is hoping to do a combined French and Law degree and would love to study abroad. She is an avid reader of fiction and poetry, enjoys music, and likes going out with her friends.

Louise Gordon is 18 and is currently finishing her 'A' levels in English, French and Music at La Swap sixth form college in North London. Louise has a long-time love of music: she sings, plays the piano and clarinet, and plans to study music at university. Her other interests include theatre, opera and literature.

Gülşen Hüseyin is 21, Turkish, and lives in North London. She is a final year Psychology student at the University of Westminster. Gülşen is a part-time poet, reads science fiction, and loves going to gigs with her friends.

Nkem Ijeh was born in London and lives in Hackney with her family. She is 21 years old and is studying English and Media Studies at Nene University, Northampton. Her hobbies include cycling, travelling, tennis, and watching TV and films. After university, she would like to become a teacher.

Melanie Knight is 18 years old and is studying Music at Durham University. Music is her passion – she sings, plays the flute and the piano, and wants to go to music college after university, to train as an opera singer.

Melanie Lewis lives in Suffolk and recently turned 18. She enjoys drama, dance, shopping, and socialising with her friends. She wants to study Performing Arts at university so that she can fulfil her dream of becoming an actress.

Kate Lloyd is 18 and lives in Hackney, East London. She is currently taking a 'gap' year – working nine-to-five then travelling round the world – before going to Leeds University to study History. She is looking forward to meeting new people and writing all those long essays!

Hara Markos is 19. She has lived in Hackney all her life, with her very large and loving family. She enjoys sport and fitness and is keen to pursue this as a career through basketball coaching and working as a personal trainer.

Alice O'Keeffe is 19 and has just started university at Kings' College, Cambridge, studying English. She hopes to spend her student loan on lots of travelling and promises she will pay it all back when she writes her first bestselling novel!

Sairra Patel was born and brought up in Hackney. She converted to Islam at 18, and is now 22. Her hobbies include reading, writing and travel. She is about to give birth to her first child.

Jennifer Rickard is 14. She was born in Chester and moved to Suffolk when she was five. She lives with her mum, dad and younger brother. Jennifer loves listening to music, is a fan of *Friends* and *Casualty*, and enjoys reading and drama.

Abigail Rozenberg is 16, and is studying English, History and Politics for her 'A' levels. She lives in West London with her parents and elder brother. Her interests include reading, painting, arguing and writing furious letters to newspapers.

Maya Selway is 21. She is studying silversmithing and metalwork at Camberwell College of Arts and after her degree, she hopes to continue her creative work. She lives in South London and loves going out there with all her friends.

Ella Ward is 13 and lives with her mum, dad and younger brother, Jack. She goes to Stowmarket High School and is mad about swimming – she trains three times a week and is on the team for her local club. She also likes other sports, spending time with her friends, and creating wacky objects!

grab a livewire!

real life, real issues, real books, real bite

Rebellion, rows, love and sex ... pushy boyfriends, fussy parents,
infuriating brothers and pests of sisters ... body image, trust, fear
and hope ... homelessness, bereavement, friends and foes ...
raves and parties, teachers and bullies ... identity, culture clash,
tension and fun ... abuse, alcoholism, cults and survival ... fat
thighs, hairy legs, hassle and angst ... music, black issues, media
and politics ... animal rights, environment, veggies and travel ...
taking risks, standing up, shouting loud and breaking out ...

... grab a Livewire!

For a free copy of our latest catalogue,
send a stamped addressed envelope to:

The Sales Department
Livewire Books
The Women's Press Ltd
34 Great Sutton Street
London EC1V 0LQ
Tel: 0171 251 3007
Fax: 0171 608 1938

Also of interest:

Charlotte Cole, editor

Between You and Me

Real-life Diaries and Letters by Women Writers

Sarra Manning of *J17* on a particularly hopeless boyfriend, Sylvia Plath on trying to win prizes, Mary Shelley on her travels through Europe and Bidisha on the trials of love and work ...

Between You and Me reveals personal diaries and letters of young women who have gone on to become successful writers. Discover their intimate thoughts, wishes and dreams. See how they juggled working hard to get what they wanted while making the space to have a good time. And learn which future women were truly wicked and wild!

Young Adult Non-fiction £4.99
ISBN 0 7043 4955 8

Jane Waghorn, editor

Through Thick and Thin

Young Women Talk Relationships

'I am not, by nature, a jealous person, so my reaction to Paul's new girlfriend astonished me . . .'

'Only recently have I begun to think of my parents as normal human beings. I'm still shocked when either of them mentions their lives before I was born.'

'Being eighteen in the nineties is tough enough, but dealing with seven demanding sisters on a daily basis adds to the challenge . . .'

Relationships. With boyfriends, parents, sisters, brothers, friends and strangers.

Relationships that work, are hard to handle, make you happy or even drive you nuts.

Better than your best friend's diary, here are the true and gripping accounts of how young women really feel about the relationships in their lives.

Young Adult Non-fiction £3.50
ISBN 0 7043 4940 X

What the judges and media have said about Livewire:

Livewire Books have won:

The Other Award
The Red Fist and Silver Slate Pencil Award
The Council on Interracial Books Award
The National Conference of Christians and Jews Mass Media Award
The Lewis Carroll Shelf Award

and much, much more.

The press has said:

'Outstanding' *Vogue*
'Stupendous' *Guardian*
'Outrageously funny' *7 Days*
'Hugely enjoyable' *British Book News*
'Compulsively witty' *Times Literary Supplement*
'Riotous and down-to-earth' *Africa World Review*
'Genuinely funny' *Los Angeles Times*
'Explosive . . . exceptional' *Times Literary Supplement*
'Brilliant' *Observer*
'Riotous' *Times Educational Supplement*